BLAZERS

SUPER SPEED

STOCK CAR
Racing

BY TRACY NELSON MAURER

Reading Consultant:
Barbara J. Fox
Professor Emerita
North Carolina State University

Content Consultant:
Donald Davidson
Historian, Indianapolis Motor Speedway
Indianapolis, Indiana

CAPSTONE PRESS
a capstone imprint

Blazers Books are published by Capstone Press,
1710 Roe Crest Drive, North Mankato, Minnesota 56003
www.capstonepub.com

Library of Congress Cataloging-in-Publication Data
Maurer, Tracy, 1965–
    Stock car racing / by Tracy Nelson Maurer.
    p. cm.—(Blazers. Super speed.)
    Includes bibliographical references and index.
    Summary: "Describes stock cars and stock car racing, including safety features
and NASCAR rules governing races"—Provided by publisher.
    ISBN 978-1-4296-9997-6 (library binding)
    ISBN 978-1-4765-1363-8 (ebook pdf)
    1. Stock car racing—Juvenile literature. I. Title.
GV1029.9.S74M3284 2013
796.72—dc23   2012033232

Editorial Credits
Aaron Sautter, editor; Kyle Grenz, designer; Eric Manske, production specialist

Photo Credits
Getty Images: Dozier Mobley/Don O'Reilly, 7; Newscom: Cal Sport Media/Ashley R Dickerson,
4-5, 9, 27, Cal Sport Media/Walter G Arce, 17, Icon SMI 144/Marc Sanchez, 20, Icon SMI 394/
Matthew O'Haren, 25, Icon SMI CBB/Dannie Walls, 29, cover, Icon SMI953/David J. Griffin, 14-15, 19;
Shutterstock: Action Sports Photography, 13, 18, 22-23, 26, Walter G Arce, 10-11

Artistic Effects
Shutterstock: 1xpert, My Portfolio, rodho

The author thanks Marty Forcier, Chuck Abrams, and Meg Maurer.

The publisher does not endorse products whose logos may appear on objects in images in this book.

Printed in the United States of America in Brainerd, Minnesota.
092012   006938BANGS13

TABLE OF CONTENTS

FAST, LOUD, AND FUN

Engines roar! Tires squeal! Fans cheer as powerful stock cars streak by. Stock car racing delivers exciting thrills on huge **superspeedways** and small local tracks.

FAST FACT

Stock car racing is the most popular sport in the United States. More fans go to stock car races than any other sport.

superspeedway —a racetrack that is at least 1.5 miles (2.4 kilometers) long

BUILDING A BETTER STOCK CAR

Early stock cars were the same as cars for sale at **dealerships**. But today's race cars are powerful machines. They are specially built for safety and speed.

FAST FACT

Bill France Sr. started the National Association for Stock Car Auto Racing (NASCAR) in 1947. NASCAR held its first race at Daytona Beach, Florida, in 1948.

The Daytona Beach Road Course hosted NASCAR races until 1958.

NASCAR created the Car of Tomorrow (COT) **specs** in 2006. All cars in the NASCAR Sprint Cup races must match COT rules. The rules help make races safer.

spec—short for specification; a spec states detailed information and instructions about how something should be built

CAR OF TOMORROW

FAST FACT

NASCAR cars don't have regular tires. They use smooth racing slicks instead. The smooth surface helps these special tires get a strong grip on the track.

COT rules require cars to have **front splitters**. These special parts slice through the air to create downward force on cars. The extra air pressure reduces speed and increases driver control.

FRONT SPLITTER

front splitter—a flat surface at the front of a stock car that creates downward pressure

COT rules add extra **cockpit**
space for safety. The extra space
creates a large **crumple zone**. In
a crash, this zone directs the force
away from the driver.

cockpit—the place where a driver sits in a race car

crumple zone—the front part of a car that is designed
to crumple and absorb some of the force of a crash

FAST FACT

NASCAR stock cars do not have doors.
COT rules made car windows larger so
drivers could easily escape through
them in an emergency.

PHOTO DIAGRAM

1. **FRONT SPLITTER**

2. **ROLL CAGE**

3. **COCKPIT**

4. **SPOILER**

5. **WINDOW NET**

6. **SLICKS**

FORD

EcoBoost

Ford

FUSION

GOODYEAR

MOOG
STEERING & SUSPENSION

MAHLE

COMP
CAMS

Edelbrock

K&N

SUNOCO

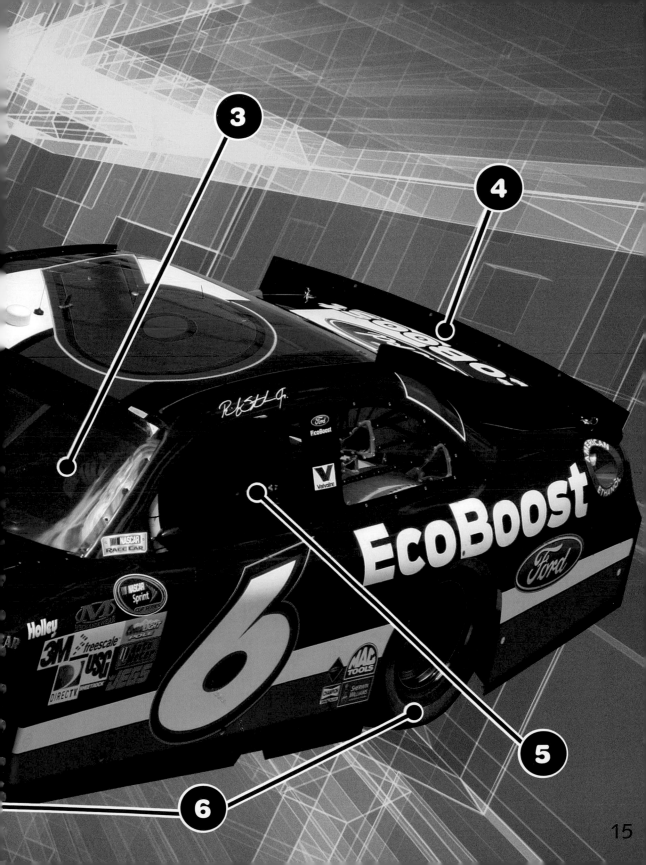

GREEN MEANS GO!

Each year the Daytona 500 kicks off the NASCAR Sprint Cup series. Drivers compete for points in 36 races during the season. At the end of the season, the driver with the most points wins the championship.

series—a group of related things or events that come one after another

FAST FACT

NASCAR began allowing small differences in car body styles in 2012. Cars still follow COT rules, but they look more like cars at dealerships again.

DAYTONA

NASCAR drivers run two **qualifying laps** before each race. The fastest lap determines if a driver can compete in the race. It also decides a driver's place in the starting lineup.

The top 43 drivers usually qualify for a NASCAR race. But past races and team standings can sometimes change the starting lineup.

Green means "go" at all auto races. But car specs, number of laps, and point systems can all be different. Different racetracks, race series, and **sanctioning bodies** all have their own rules.

FAST FACT

The National Stock Car Racing Commission governs NASCAR races. The NASCAR rule book is more than 100 pages long.

sanctioning body—a group or organization that sets rules and governs results

Most stock car races run **counterclockwise** on oval tracks. NASCAR Sprint Cup series races are 300 to 600 miles (483 to 966 km) long. Drivers usually complete hundreds of laps to finish a race.

counterclockwise—the opposite direction than the hands of a clock move

Race teams work together to win races. NASCAR crew chiefs plan **strategies** for the race. Spotters watch the race from a high view. They look for openings to help drivers take the lead.

strategy—a plan for winning a race

Crew chiefs use radios to help guide drivers during races.

Drivers bring their cars into pit stalls for service during a race. NASCAR pit crews work fast. They change tires, add fuel, and fix broken parts all in less than 30 seconds.

FAST FACT

Trained pit crews use only two or three power tools during a pit stop.

MORE THRILLS AHEAD

Stock cars continue to improve. Future cars will drive faster and keep drivers safer. Stock car racing will provide fans with high speed excitement for years to come!

FAST FACT

In 2007 a Dodge Charger built to NASCAR specs set a new land speed record. It drove 247 miles (398 km) per hour at the Bonneville Salt Flats in Utah.

GLOSSARY

cockpit (KOK-pit)—the place where a driver sits in a race car

counterclockwise (koun-tur-KLAHK-wize)—the opposite direction than the hands of a clock move

crumple zone (KRUMP-uhl ZOHN)—the front part of a car that is designed to crumple and absorb some of the force of a crash to help protect the driver

dealership (DEE-lur-ship)—a place where people buy cars

front splitter (FRUNT SPLIT-ur)—a flat surface at the front of a stock car that creates downward pressure

qualifying lap (KWAH-luh-fye-ing LAP)—a timed lap drivers run before a race to earn a starting spot in the race

santioning body (SANGK-shun-ing BOD-ee)—a group or organization that sets rules and governs results

series (SIHR-eez)—a group of related things or events that come one after another

spec (SPEK)—short for specification; a spec states detailed information and instructions about how something should be built

strategy (STRAT-uh-jee)—a plan for winning a race

superspeedway (soo-pur-SPEED-way)—a racetrack that is at least 1.5 miles (2.4 kilometers) long

READ MORE

David, Jack. *Stock Cars.* Cool Rides. Minneapolis: Bellwether Media, 2008.

Francis, Jim. *Stock Car Secrets.* NASCAR. New York: Crabtree Pub. Co., 2008.

Mason, Paul. *Stock Cars.* Motorsports. Mankato, Minn.: Amicus, 2011.

INTERNET SITES

FactHound offers a safe, fun way to find Internet sites related to this book. All of the sites on FactHound have been researched by our staff.

Here's all you do:

Visit *www.facthound.com*

Type in this code: 9781429699976

 Check out projects, games and lots more at www.capstonekids.com

INDEX